The Complete Riding and Driving System
BOOK 6

Lungeing

*The Official Handbook of The
German National Equestrian Federation*

Published in 1990 in the United States of America by
Half Halt Press Inc, 6416 Burkittsville Road,
Middletown, Maryland 21769

© FN-Verlag der Deutschen Reiterlichen Vereinigung
GmbH approves this edition of 'Richtlinien für Reiten
und Fahren, Band 6

English language edition © 1990 The Kenilworth Press Limited

Translation by **Gisela Holstein**
Consultant **Jane Kidd**

Phototypeset by DMD Ltd, St Clements, Oxford

Printed in Great Britain by The Bath Press, Avon

Library of Congress Cataloging in Publication Data

The complete riding and driving system.
 Translation of: Richtlinien für Reiten und Fahren.
 Includes indexes.
 Contents: Bk. 1. The principles of riding
 – bk. 2. Advanced techniques for riding – [etc.]
 – bk. 6. Lungeing.
 I. Deutsche Reiterliche Vereinigung.
SF309.R53413   1987   798.2'4'0943   90–39292
ISBN 0–939481–04–9 (v. 4)

Contents

Foreword

Years ago, the principles of lungeing technique were passed on by word of mouth from generation to generation. Today, short-cuts are sometimes taken, on account of the faster pace of life and the greater financial pressures of dealing with horses. These guidelines give the trainer and the interested rider an opportunity to familiarise themselves with the theory of lungeing, and then to put it into practice.

We are sure that this book, Volume 6 of the Complete Riding and Driving System, will be welcomed by trainers and riders alike.

German National Equestrian Federation
Sports Division
Warendorf, Westphalia

1. Introduction

Lungeing is exercising, gymnasticising and/or training young or experienced horses on a rein approximately 7 m long.

It is an excellent way of getting young horses used to tack and regular work, and of teaching them to trust humans. This trust, however, can only be achieved if the lungeing is executed correctly. Incorrect lungeing can spoil a horse's confidence forever.

If a trainer has 'feel' and the right psychological approach, work on the lunge can be very beneficial indeed. It can create lasting impressions in the horse's mind and can build up confidence in the trainer better than most other training methods.

When handling an unspoilt horse, force of any kind must be avoided; but if a spoilt horse knows his strength and uses it to resist, the lunge can show him quickly who is in charge.

For no matter what reason the lunge is used, its highest value lies in the psychological aspect.

Trust and respect are the foundation of a successful education, and the lunge is a powerful means of achieving this. It smoothes the path for the training under the saddle – firstly by achieving '*Losgelassenheit*' (suppleness combined with looseness and a complete absence of tension), but also by making up for faults in the horse's conformation or faults and problems which might have developed during training under saddle.

Real success will only come when the trainer or rider is experienced and tactful enough to adjust the work programme to the horse's needs. He must know (a) when to stop and (b) that although the lunge can help a lot, it cannot cure everything. Even the most successful lungeing can never replace training under the rider.

Horse experts, practical and theoretical, have devised a multitude of lungeing methods and auxiliary reins, which enable even the average trainer to achieve some results with the lunge. Nevertheless, the average trainer is well advised to keep his lungeing programme at a good basic level, improving the horse's *Losgelassenheit* and gymnasticising the horse's neck and back muscles.

It is necessary to be aware of the fact that the lunge can easily be turned into a forceful instrument. It should therefore be used only by persons with patience and self-discipline, who are constantly trying to improve their knowledge.

Bearing the above points in mind it is possible to summarise the independent uses of the lunge as follows:

☐ Familiarising young horses in the backing period with the saddle or driving harness.

☐ Supplementing the ordinary training programme of riding and driving horses.

☐ Compensating for any conformation faults which could become problematic during training.

☐ Re-schooling spoilt riding or driving horses.

☐ Exercising horses after an illness or rest period.

☐ In the advanced stages of training, a horse can be prepared for a higher degree of collection on a single or double lunge. In high school training the horse can be prepared for difficult movements including work in the 'pillars'.

2. Lungeing equipment

In order to achieve success in lungeing it is necessary to know what equipment is available and how to use it.

2.1 Where to lunge

The basic necessity is a suitable place in which to lunge the horse. A location must be chosen where the horse can concentrate, and the going and surroundings must be safe so that the horse does not suffer any damage. The following points must therefore be taken into consideration:

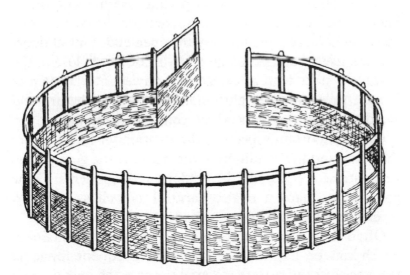

1. Suitable fencing for an outdoor lungeing ring.

☐ The circle in which the horse is working must never be smaller than 12 m in diameter.

☐ The circle or lungeing ring should have a suitable surrounding fence.

☐ The going should be springy, but not too deep.

Lungeing horses repeatedly on a circle smaller than 12 m in diameter can cause permanent damage to the horse's joints and bones: especially the fetlock joint, which is hinged and therefore is not designed to turn sideways. Lungeing on too small a circle causes swollen joints, side-bone and navicular disease.

At the beginning, horses instinctively resist work on a tight circle. They fall out over the shoulder or go on more than one track, which increases the stress on the joints.

For safety's sake, a full-size circle only should be used, and to get the most out of the lungeing it is important to have a surrounding fence.

Where circumstances do not permit a permanent lungeing ring, you can improvise by lungeing in the corner of an indoor school, fencing off only the open end. Out of doors you can use a bank or hedge on two sides and close in the other two sides with straw bales or fence material such as blocks, poles and uprights. Set these out with care and avoid any sharp corners which could hurt the horse.

Other important aspects of the location for lungeing are the going and the condition of the track. If the going is too deep, stress is put upon the tendons and ligaments. If the going is too hard it is also harmful as well as slippery, especially when the horse is shod.

Often the lungeing surface is not properly maintained, which can be harmful to the horse. Frequent lungeing tends to shift the surface material towards the outside, and after a while the actual track is at a slant, higher on the outside and lower on the inside. The horse is then continually working on a slanted surface. The uneven pressure on the fetlock joints, tendons and ligaments is very damaging. The track should therefore be levelled after every lungeing session.

The following are suitable locations for lungeing:

☐ A permanent covered lungeing ring, such as may be found in riding schools, stud farms and training centres. The working area should have a diameter of between 12 and 16 m. Such a ring is the most suitable place in which to work a young horse. If the ring is also intended to be used for riding or vaulting, 16 m is the minimum diameter.

☐ An indoor arena measuring a minimum of 15 × 30 m provides ample space for lungeing, provided that the school is not used for riding at the same time. Lunge at one end with a temporary fence at the open end. The same applies to outdoor arenas. Lungeing and riding at the same time are only possible if the arena is large enough to prevent the horses from interfering with each other. A barrier between the horse on the lunge and ridden horses is advisable for safety reasons.

☐ Lungeing young horses in an outdoor manège can be difficult because of outside distractions. When lungeing experienced horses, however, it is not so important always to have a totally quiet, peaceful atmosphere. In fact it can be a mistake to work horses for too long in sheltered surroundings as it can make them very susceptible to outside influences.

☐ A permanent outdoor lungeing ring with a suitable surrounding is the ideal location. It allows concentrated work on the lunge without interference from other horses, and at the same time the horse learns to work in a natural atmosphere, which is a better preparation for shows, etc.

The disadvantage of outdoor lungeing is the weather and its influence on the going.

If you want to jump the horse on the lunge, space permitting, you can use the area surrounding the ring to arrange a track with cavaletti or one or two small fences.

2.2 Basic equipment and its use

The choice of lungeing equipment depends on factors such as what you are trying to achieve with lungeing, the type of horse, and your own experience.

We will deal first with basic lungeing equipment. Special equipment is dealt with later when the various aims of the work on the lunge are explained.

When lungeing during the backing period, the horse

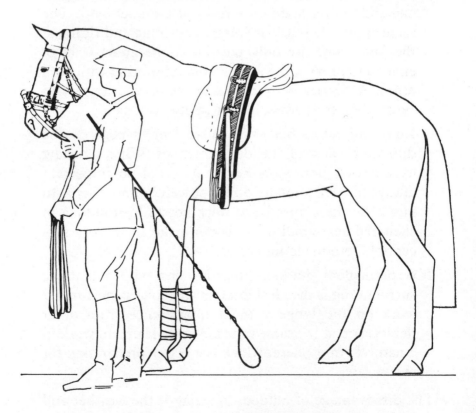

2. The basic lungeing equipment.

should be tacked up with saddle and snaffle bridle as early as possible.

In addition you will need:

☐ A lunge-rein, approximately 7 m long.

☐ A whip, long enough to actually touch the horse with the end of the thong while lungeing.

☐ A pair of side-reins.

It is advisable to use a roller or lungeing surcingle over the saddle. The roller should have D-rings at intervals on each side, which enable you to attach the side-reins at varying heights.

Through ignorance, or simply because it involves less work, some people lunge horses in just a roller and without a saddle. This allows the roller a certain mobility, which limits the effectiveness of the side-reins. The missing weight on the horse's back also diminishes the effect of the lungeing. For whatever other reasons horses are lunged, the main one will always be to make the horse's back work. The activity of the hind legs leads to a rhythmical movement of the back muscles which will be stimulated and increased by the additional weight of the saddle. Without the weight of a saddle the work on the lunge is not really effective and is more or less just exercising on the lunge.

For similar reasons a proper bridle should be used, even with a cavesson. Lungeing a horse off a headcollar is not correct and can lead to many problems. A headcollar cannot be fitted as firmly as a cavesson and will slip around the horse's head and can injure the eye.

When lungeing, you want to make the horse supple and relaxed. Relaxation starts in the poll and parotid gland area. The bit in the horse's mouth stimulates the saliva flow, which in turn relaxes the muscles of the parotid glands and supples the poll.

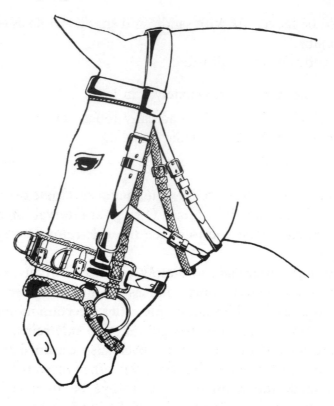

3. Correctly fitted bridle and cavesson.

The bridle should be used without the reins and should be fitted with a thick, loose-ring snaffle bit. The use of a drop noseband is recommended as it prevents the horse from setting the jaw – which usually happens when lungeing with an ordinary noseband, as the bit is allowed to move too loosely in the mouth. A grakle noseband is not recommended as too much pressure can be put on to the nasal bone when the upper noseband is pulled down by the lower strap. Used together with a cavesson, the drop noseband has the added advantage of lying below the cavesson's noseband, and it therefore does not interfere with it.

If a normal bridle is used with reins, these have to be

twisted under the horse's neck and secured with the throat lash. Alternatively, the reins can be left loose, but they must then be threaded through the ring on top of the roller.

Boots or bandages should be used to prevent injury to the legs.

The lunge is a tubular web rein, 2 cm wide and at least 7 m long. At one end it has a 20 cm loop for holding the lunge. At the other end is either a hook or a buckle fastening. The more practical of the two is a lightweight hook; if a buckle fastening is used it must be easy to handle, which means that the buckle has to be oval-shaped and large, and the holes have to be big.

Note that a leather lunge tends to become too slippery when wet. Equally unsatisfactory are leather grips on the hand piece of the lunge – which although they prevent the lunge from slipping through the hand, can cause severe injuries to the hand. A swivel joint can help to untwist the lunge.

The lunge whip is a very important piece of equipment. The stock should be 1.8 2 m long, light in weight, flexible but not too floppy. The thong, which is secured to the stock by means of a loop or keeper, should be 3 m long, so that the trainer – with arm stretched – is able to touch the horse with the end of it. The hand piece and the first third of the stock must be heavy enough to balance the rest of the whip, including the thong. Only then can you use the whip properly. For the same reason, it is necessary to keep the thong soft and tangle free.

The lungeing whip should never be used to punish a horse – it is an aid without which it is impossible to train the horse correctly. The correct use of the whip has to be practised, as it is very difficult at first to manoeuvre the end of the long thong accurately.

Many people make do with too short a whip, but without adequate equipment you cannot achieve a good result, and lungeing without an effective whip is like riding without legs.

The roller is usually made of jute, with leather binding. All-leather rollers are very expensive and need a lot of maintenance.

Since the roller is used over the saddle, for most horses it should be approximately 2 m long in total – the actual roller 1.5 m and the leather straps 50 cm.

Pads on both sides of the withers are necessary if the roller is to be used without a saddle, e.g. when exercising the horse. The roller is fitted with Ds (at least three pairs) half way down each side, at intervals of about 5 cm. Thus the side-reins can be adjusted at different heights. In the centre of the top part of the roller is an additional ring, to which a check-rein (see page 48) may be attached. This ring is situated close to the front edge of the roller. Near the back edge of the top of the roller is another ring, to which a crupper may be fitted. The underside of the roller and the fastenings must be padded, so as not to damage the saddle or the horse.

While lungeing, it is advisable to remove the stirrups and leathers; otherwise they must be rolled up and secured under the roller so that they cannot damage the saddle.

Side-reins are a necessary part of the lungeing equipment. There are many different types available, but not all of them are suitable for all horses.

The most common is the plain leather side-rein 1.5 m in length. The side-rein connects the bit ring with the side of the roller or girth. A lightweight hook is the most practical attachment to the bit ring. At the other end, the side-rein has a long strap with several holes and an easy-to-handle buckle.

Some side-reins have elasticated inserts – such as a rubber ring or elasticated webbing – to soften the effect of the side-reins. These are not recommended. The additional weight of the rubber ring disturbs the action of the bit in the mouth.

Running reins may be used instead of side-reins. These consist of two web or leather reins, each 2.5–2.75 m long. Each running rein is threaded through the bit ring, and both ends are then attached to the roller.

Boots and other leg protection are essential, as the horse moves on a relatively small circle, which can cause brushing. The forelegs should be fitted with brushing boots or bandages. Brushing boots with buckles or Velcro fastenings are easy to put on and labour-saving. Bandages are nice and soft on the horse's legs, especially when made from a soft, thick material. The hind legs may be protected with ankle boots.

The drawback of all leg protectors is the fact that they interfere with the free movement of the tendon and with blood circulation. Cold hosing immediately after exercise is therefore advisable.

The cavesson should be made from good-quality leather. The well-padded metal noseplate operates on the nasal bone and, through it, also on the poll. On the metal noseplate up to three rings are fitted, to which the lunge rein can be attached. Generally, the centre one is chosen. Two throat lashes secure the position of the cavesson and prevent it being pulled across the face of the horse, causing damage to the eye. The noseband is rather heavy because of the weight of the metal noseplate. With the additional weight of the lunge, it could slip down and press on the horse's nostrils, but to prevent this, an additional leather strap, connecting the centre of the

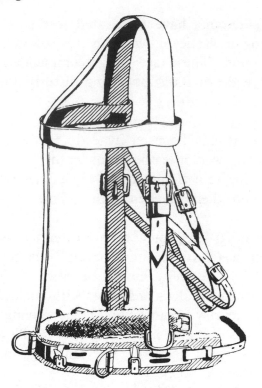

4. Cavesson.

noseband to the centre of the headpiece, is often fitted. The height of the noseband is adjusted so that it lies between the jawbone and the corners of the mouth, touching neither of them.

On either side of the headpiece are two rings through which a check-rein can be fed.

Rings on the bottom end of the cheekpieces allow a bit to be attached whenever the cavesson is to be used without a bridle.

In general, a simple snaffle bridle is used with the cavesson. The cavesson noseband then lies *under* the bridle where it will not interfere with the free movement of the bit rings and cheekpieces, and the cavesson headpiece and throat lashes lie *over* the bridle.

As well as the basic lungeing equipment described there are many – sometimes grotesque – variations and additions. A good trainer, however, will try to use only a bare minimum of equipment, and will employ auxiliary reins only if necessary and for a limited period of time.

2.3 Cavesson or bridle?

Attaching the lunge rein
When lungeing, you have to make a decision as to whether to attach the lunge to the cavesson or to the bit ring. This decision will depend on the horse's stage of training and whether you are:

☐ Lungeing a young horse in the first, familiarising phase.

☐ Gymnasticising a horse as part of his basic training as a riding horse.

☐ Lungeing or working in-hand to achieve a higher degree of collection.

During the first phase of training the lunge should be attached to the cavesson. In this phase the side-reins should be loosely adjusted. The cavesson can be a light one with only a central ring on the metal plate, but it must be well secured with the two throat lashes, to prevent eye injuries.

As already mentioned, substitutes such as ordinary headcollars or nosebands are not advisable and will diminish the achievements of the lunge work.

If there is no cavesson available and you *have* to make do with a substitute, a bridle with a sturdy drop noseband should be chosen and the lunge should be attached to both the bit ring and the cheekpiece of the noseband.

The use of a coupling, connecting the two bit rings, has a bad influence: when the lunge is attached to the

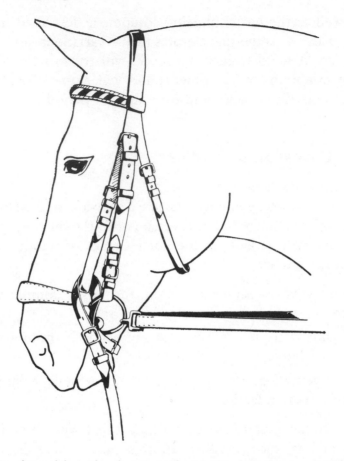

5. Attaching the lunge rein to the bit ring and the cheekpiece of the noseband.

coupling's centre ring, it exerts more pressure on the outside bit ring and gives the snaffle a nutcracker action, its joint pressing on the upper palate.

If the lunge has a buckle fastening, attach it in such a way that the tongue of the buckle faces away from the horse and so cannot possibly injure it.

Depending on the type of horse and the practical experience of the trainer, even in this initial phase of training a young horse can wear a bridle under the cavesson. But the lunge should be attached to the cavesson's centre

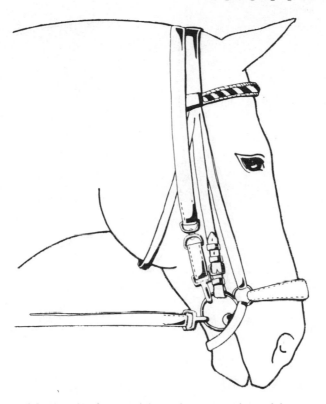

*6. Method of attaching the over-head lunge,
viewed from the outside.*

ring, not to the bit ring. The bit should be raised slightly,
for if it hangs low in the mouth, the horse could develop a
tongue problem.

At a later stage, when the horse is used to being lunged,
you can omit the cavesson and work directly off the bridle.
However, when attaching the lunge to the bit there is
always a danger that the bit can be pulled through the
mouth, which must be avoided. This can create a lot of
difficulties, such as tongue problems or stiffness in the
poll. As a safeguard, therefore, side-reins should be used
to keep the bit steady in the mouth, and they should be
adjusted in such a way that the outside side-rein forms a
counter-weight to the lunge on the inside bit ring. What-

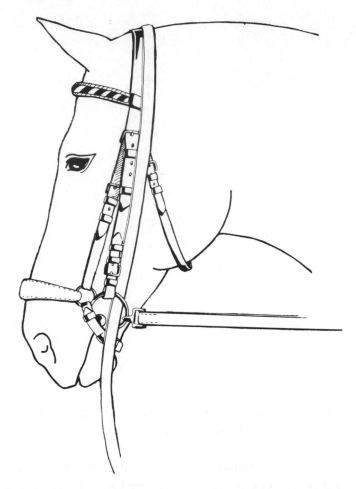

*7. Path of the 'over-head' lunge, viewed
from the inside.*

ever the stage of training, though, the less-experienced
trainer should avoid lungeing off the bit, and should
attach the lunge to the bit ring and the cheekpiece of the
noseband, as shown in Fig. 5.

Only experts at lungeing should use the lunge adjusted
'over head', whereby the lunge is hooked on to the outside
bit ring and runs over the horse's poll, through the inside
bit ring to the trainer's hand.

This method of attaching the lunge has the same effect as a gag bridle: the corners of the mouth are pulled upwards by the bit, raising the horse's head and neck. Very occasionally a horse might need an even more intensive 'raising effect', in which case one would lunge the horse with a check-rein.

For experienced handlers the 'sliding' lunge can also prove useful in certain cases. If you intend to use this method you will need a round-stitched lunge line or a clothesline, made free-running with a bar of soap.

There are three different ways of attaching the sliding lunge, depending on what you want to achieve:

□ For better flexion and slight raising of the horse's front, the sliding lunge is first hooked on to the outside bit

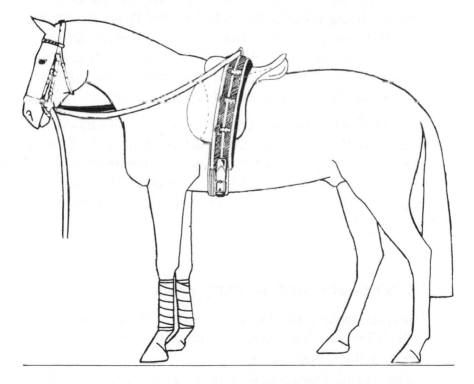

8. The sliding lunge.

ring. From there it is fed through the ring on top of the roller and back to the horse's head, but this time through the inside bit ring and thence to the trainer's hand (see Fig. 8). This gives the trainer greater control over the horse's lateral bend.

☐ To increase collection the sliding lunge is hooked on to the inside bit ring, then fed through the ring on top of the roller and passed from the outside towards the inside through both bit rings, underneath the horse's head and back into the trainer's hand.

☐ For horses which tend to fall out over the shoulder and bend their neck laterally inwards too much, becoming 'loose in front of the withers', the third method of attaching the sliding lunge can help. Pass the rein through the inside bit ring to the ring on top of the roller, bring it down through the outside bit ring and from there under the horse's head directly to the trainer's hand. This helps to straighten the horse as it controls the outside shoulder and creates collection if used together with forward-driving whip aids.

With the sliding lunge the trainer's hand can, like a rider's hand, yield the rein or give a half-halt to regulate the pace. The hand can be soft and yielding or non-allowing.

Therefore side-reins are totally omitted in this kind of lungeing work, as they would interfere with the actions of the trainer's hand.

2.4 Side-reins and auxiliary reins

Side-reins connect the horse's mouth with the roller or girth. They position the horse's head and neck in whatever way the trainer decides.

The use of side-reins is frequently thought to be the reason for the often criticised fact that some German-trained horses seem to be made too short in the neck. The incorrect use of side-reins sometimes provides an outline which seems to support this criticism – and strengthens the arguments of those trainers who support the idea of the horse moving in total freedom.

The German system takes the view that man can only use the horse as a weight carrier, without harming his health, if the horse's muscles and balance are prepared for the unnatural burden of the rider's weight and the pressures involved when being used as a riding or driving horse.

This preparation and adaptation to the new life necessitates a change in posture (shape). This change is only possible if the horse, after the initial stage of training, seeks and accepts a springy contact with the bit. Only after quite a lengthy period of gymnasticising work can the horse's working posture develop into 'self carriage'.

Therefore the German system does not adhere to the 'Natural Training Method', whose followers maintain that self carriage in a trained horse can only be achieved by gentle familiarisation.

One of the means to achieve and establish self carriage are the side-reins.

When lungeing, various methods of employing side-reins can be used, depending on the reason for which the horse is being trained or gymnasticised.

The ordinary side-rein, depending on the degree of training, enables the horse, to find contact with the bit. Using the poll, and the chest, jaw and neck muscles, the horse tucks in his head by 'giving' in the parotid gland area. This is achieved without a shortening of the neck, but with a gradually higher carriage of neck and poll. This submissive bending and giving in the poll is called '*Beizaeumung*' – 'submission' – at the poll.

To achieve submission in basic training the side-reins

are attached to the roller at such a height that the horse's mouth is at approximately the same level as the point of his shoulder.

When the horse is a little more advanced and collection is beginning, with lowering of the haunches, the horse's mouth should be at approximately the same height as his hip bones.

The length of the side-reins should be adjusted so that during initial work the horse's nasal bone is at least the width of one hand in front of the vertical, and with advanced work nearly vertical. The trainer can judge this only when the horse is moving and is in front of the forward driving aids.

Attaching the side-reins when they have been shortened must be done with great care. Always fasten the outside side-rein first and then, very carefully, the inside rein. One careless move can jeopardise the work for quite some time.

During work on the lunge the trainer must always remember that the horse should go forward into the outside rein, and then, through submission in the poll, become light on it (or in German: 'bounce back off it'). Therefore it is wrong to use side-reins with additional 'puffers' in the shape of rubber rings. As the rein is slightly elasticated, the horse learns to poke against the bit; when ridden, he will poke against the rider's hand, and will not learn to submit in the poll.

During the initial training period – after the familiarising phase – the horse has to learn to seek contact with the outside rein by stretching the outside of his entire body. The use of ordinary side-reins, of equal length on both sides, is therefore recommended. At this stage it is too early to try to give the horse lateral flexion and bend by shortening the inside side-rein. The inside hind leg is not yet gymnasticised enough. As a result the horse will become hollow in the neck and body and will fall on to the outside shoulder.

Even as the training becomes a little more advanced it is still preferable not to shorten the inside side-rein but rather to try to achieve flexion by correct use of the lunge and forward driving aids.

Horses who try to lean on the bit in spite of sufficiently long side-reins, tend to go too deep. Do not be tempted to adjust the side-reins to a higher ring on the roller because the horse will lean on the bit even more. The correct remedy is to push the horse more forward into a freer pace at the correct moment and thus make him come back off the bit.

If a horse carries his head too high and does not want to come down on to the bit, do not try to force the head down by moving the side-reins to a lower ring on the roller. This downwards pull causes the horse to pull upwards against it. The solution here is to adjust the side-reins slightly higher, keep the horse straighter and slow down the pace, while lungeing on a smaller circle. In most cases this will correct the fault.

As a rule, tying a horse's head down will only create an illusion of success. Sometimes people try to tie the head down with running reins or side-reins attached to the roller between the horse's forelegs. Horses who are tied down like this go with too deep a head position and with a high croup. The hind legs are unable to bend and cannot come more underneath the body. The back becomes tense and cannot move with any spring or elasticity. Tying down a horse's head in this way must therefore be avoided – apart from in a few isolated cases where it may become necessary for a short period of time.

Before every lungeing session the trainer must check the length of the side-reins: counting the holes is not sufficient, neither is measuring by eye. The correct and safe method is to stand in front of the horse, touch both ends of the bit with the index or middle finger and pull gently forward to feel if the tension is equal.

The Lauffer rein

This is a piece of lungeing equipment named after a dressage trainer from around the beginning of this century. It is a type of rein which does not have the disadvantages of ordinary side-reins, which can only act in one direction and become tighter when the horse tries to change the position of his head and neck. The Lauffer rein is of benefit to horses which are tight in the back, have too high a head carriage and cannot find the way forward and down. This double rein invites the head to slide forward

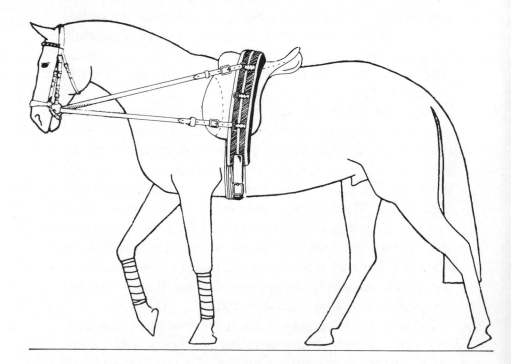

9. The Lauffer rein.

and downwards and gives the horse more freedom of movement.

At first the ends of the Lauffer rein are attached to the middle and lowest rings on the roller, and at a later stage of training to the middle or highest rings on the side of the roller and the centre ring on top of the roller.

Both the ordinary side-rein and the Lauffer rein stabilise the base of the neck by sideways restriction.

The following auxiliary reins do not have this advantage and should only be used in special cases and by expert trainers.

The Chambon

This is used predominantly in France and Italy, where it is employed mainly in the training of show jumpers. The Chambon works on the horse's poll, creating maximum arching of the back and allowing unlimited freedom for the horse's nose to move forward and downwards, strengthening the muscles concerned. The moment the horse lowers his head and neck, the Chambon becomes ineffective. The horse then moves in a low outline, without contact with the bit and without any sideways restriction.

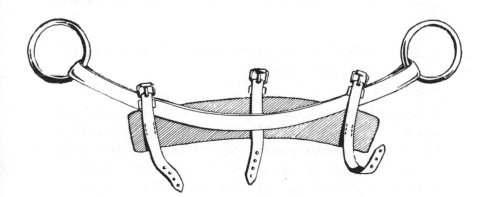

10. Headpiece of the Chambon.

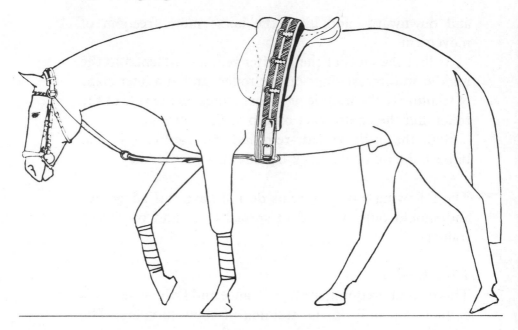

11. The effect of the Chambon.

The Chambon consists of:

☐ A headpiece, with a ring at each end. This is fitted on top of the headpiece of the bridle.

☐ An ordinary side-rein, which runs between the forelegs to the girth.

☐ A piece of nylon cord, approximately 1.35 m long, with a snap-on hook at each end.

If adjusted correctly the Chambon is only felt by the horse when he raises his head. He then feels gentle pressure on the poll and, simultaneously, the bit moves upwards in the mouth. To avoid the pressure on the poll, the horse lowers his head and neck and the Chambon reins hang loose, without any effect.

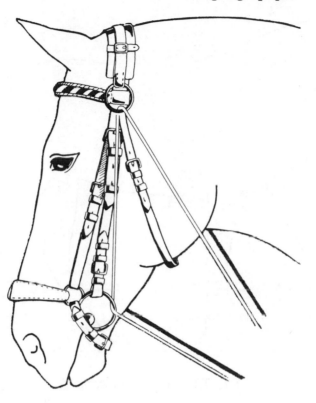

12. How to attach the Gogue.

The Gogue

A similar rein is the 'Gogue', developed in France. Here
the nylon cord is not hooked on to the bit rings, but is fed
through the bit rings and hooked back into a clip so that it
forms a triangle between the horse's chest, poll and
mouth. This means that the movement on the bit is
upwards-backwards, as opposed to the upward action of
the Chambon.

As with the Chambon, there is a danger of the horse
falling out over the shoulder and therefore it should be
used only in a lungeing ring.

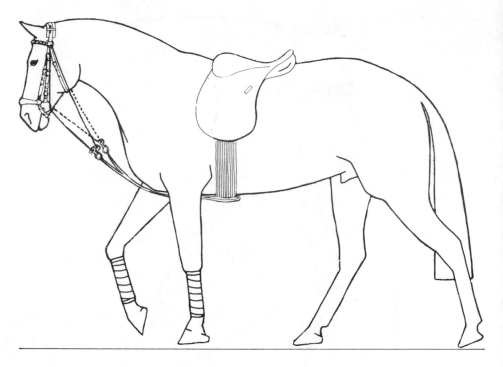

13. The Gogue in action.

The standing martingale

This is another restriction that can be worn when lunge-ing. The standing martingale is a simple leather strap (side-rein) which is attached to the roller underneath the horse, and runs between the forelegs towards the head, where it is hooked on to the noseband or attached via a coupling to the bit rings.

The standing martingale prevents the horse from rais-ing his head, but does not invite a contact or apply any sideways restriction. Its training value when lungeing is, therefore, very limited.

Whenever a standing martingale is fitted, it is advisable also to use a neck strap from a running martingale, otherwise the horse could get his foot caught when lowering his head.

3. How to lunge

3.1 Use of equipment

It is essential that the trainer knows how to use the equipment correctly as only then can he hope to achieve work of value and tailor lungeing programmes to suit individual horses' requirements.

3.1.1 The lunge

When lungeing on the left rein the trainer's left hand holds the lunge, and vice versa. Any slack line is held, without twists, in neat loops approximately 30 cm long, in that same hand.

The lunge leaves the hand over the index finger, the thumb pressing down to keep the lunge firmly in the hand. There should always be some lunge line to spare in the trainer's hand to allow a little 'give' should the horse suddenly plunge or jump. Do not hold the lunge by the hand loop only, because the horse can easily jerk the lunge out of your hand, injuring your arm or fingers.

The trainer should always have an even, soft contact with the horse's mouth. He should therefore hold his hand upright, thumb uppermost, without turning in his hand excessively. The lower arm, the back of the hand and the lunge should form one straight line pointing towards the horse's mouth.

The lunge line should guide the horse and maintain the flexion in the poll. Therefore it is advisable to keep the hand holding the lunge a little in advance of the horse's mouth. This is possible if the trainer holds his elbow against his body and turns his lower arm a little sideways in the direction of movement. Also the arm will tire less quickly if held close to the body.

It is not correct to hold the lunge in the same way as holding the rein when riding. This creates in the hand a backward-pulling influence. Sometimes people use this method when training for vaulting, but even then there is no need for it.

The trainer transmits the aids on the lunge by giving and taking. This is achieved through flexing the wrist joint and if necessary, the whole arm. Short, sharp half-halts can be achieved by shaking the lunge in 'waves'. To create these waves, the trainer moves his hand quickly up and down three or four times. The waves flow towards the horse and are felt in the noseband of the cavesson, or in the bit when lunged off the bridle.

Common faults when handling the lunge

Stiff hand and arm
The hand on the lunge is held with a stiff straight arm, or the wrist joint is stiff, or the hand is held too high, which all make it difficult to 'feel' and disturb the horse's rhythm.

The lunge is too loose and trails on the ground
A trailing lunge is dangerous for the trainer, as he can become entangled in the loops. Also, the lunge, dragging on the ground, is heavy in the horse's mouth.

Contact constantly too tight
Taking a 'dead' pull on the lunge tempts a horse to lean against the pull, sometimes with all his might. As a result the rhythm, relaxation and lateral bend of the horse are all disturbed.

A lunge which is sometimes a little loose is preferable to one that is constantly too tight.

Gathering the lunge incorrectly
If the lunge is gathered incorrectly, one cannot pay out the lunge quickly or smoothly enough when the horse is moving off. A lunge which is gathered untidily is dangerous and can, if there is an emergency, cost the trainer his hand, or give the horse too hard a jerk in the mouth. The loops should lie neatly on top of one another so that they can slide out freely when the hand is opened slightly.

When shortening the lunge the loops should be gathered equally smoothly and put back into the hand, one on top of the other.

If a young horse takes fright and runs off, the hand can easily receive a friction burn. To avoid this, gloves should be worn when lungeing, but since they do mean that there is less feel in the hand, experienced trainers sometimes prefer not to wear them when they decide it is safe to go without.

Trainer changing position constantly
The trainer has to remain in the same position in the centre of the circle in order to be able to maintain a steady contact. His upper body should be turned slightly in the direction of the movement. Getting left behind with the shoulder makes the lungeing more difficult. Moving the position constantly is disturbing for the horse.

3.1.2 The whip

One of the most important parts of lungeing equipment is a well-made whip. To lunge without a whip is a waste of time, as it is like riding without forward-driving leg aids.

If used incorrectly it disturbs and frightens the horse.

When lungeing on the left rein, the whip is carried in the right hand, and vice versa. The whip is carried so that it balances comfortably in the hand and is secured by the thumb. The index finger is positioned around the stock, helping to direct the thong movement. The point of the whip is aimed towards the horse's hock; the thong is dragged along the ground. An experienced trainer can hold the end of the thong in the whip hand, letting go whenever necessary.

Most horses which are used to lungeing respect a slight raising of the whip's point as a forward-driving aid.

It is advisable to practise using the lunge whip well before it is used on a horse. With a slight turn of the wrist joint the end of the thong can be flicked in any direction. The trainer has to have a very good aim and be able to touch exactly any spot with the end of the thong. Once having mastered the technique, the trainer can touch the horse's hind leg at any given height. He can tap the hock and create more activity; he can keep the horse out on the circular track by pointing it towards the shoulder or ribcage. If a horse is nervous and going too fast, he can point the whip away from the horse, behind him, for a while. But the whip should never be omitted altogether: every horse gets used to the whip and learns to respect it as an aid.

The whip should never be used to hit or punish the horse; and cracking the whip loudly can frighten the horse and damage his trust in the aid. Rough handling can damage the whip itself, and if the whip is in poor condition the trainer cannot work effectively.

Faults in handling the whip

Lack of practice in using the whip
Using the thong silently and with perfect aim requires

practice. Only experience will prove which whip is the easiest to use. If a trainer does not use the whip correctly, he can frighten his horse and make him less able to learn during the lungeing sessions.

Placing the whip on the ground
Many people acquire the bad habit of dropping the whip on the ground, whenever they need their hands free to do other things, like adjust tack etc. A whip lying on the ground is easily broken – the horse could step on it or the trainer could stumble over it. But a greater danger is that many horses spook when the trainer bends down to pick up the whip. The frightened horse might kick and injure the trainer as a result. Therefore, whenever free hands are needed while lungeing, the whip should be put under the upper arm, pointing backwards and downwards. The trainer should make this a habit, as it is the only safe way to work.

3.1.3 The voice

The voice has an important part to play in lungeing and is considered to be a 'supporting' aid. It can have a calming or encouraging influence. The tone of the voice is more effective than the actual word uttered, but horses can, however, learn the meaning of certain words and, for example, will canter on the command 'Canter' and slow down on the word 'Whoa'. The important factor is that the trainer and/or assistant uses the same tone of voice and is consistent in his commands.

The value of the voice, however, should not be over-estimated. Horses who follow all commands promptly, like well-trained circus animals, may be obedient but in gymnastic exercises this obedience is only of limited worth. The trainer has to realise that the voice aid must always be used in conjunction with the lunge and the whip aid.

Faults in using the voice

Voice used too often and too loud
This makes some horses immune and dull; other horses become upset and lose their trust and concentration.

The voice should either animate the horse with shorter, sharper commands, or calm it with a lower tone and long-drawn-out vowels.

Too little use of voice
This prohibits a closer contact between horse and man, and with that flowing and smooth transitions.

Outside assistance
Vocal assistance from persons other than the trainer must be avoided at all costs because the horse will not concentrate on his trainer.

4. Lungeing horses at different levels of training

4.1 Lungeing trained horses

The procedure for lungeing a trained horse can be sub-divided into the following stages:

☐ Leading the horse up to the lungeing ring.

☐ Preparation for the lungeing session and attaching the side-reins.

☐ Starting to lunge.

☐ Changing the rein.

☐ Finishing the lungeing session.

The trainer should be familiar with the technique of lungeing in its various phases, and should be able to alter them according to the individual needs of each horse. The preparation and beginning of the lungeing is important as it sets the tone for the session. If basic mistakes are made, their effects sometimes only become noticeable at a later stage. Haste and tension, unprepared arenas, forgotten tools which have to be sent for are examples of a poor approach to the work. The conscientious trainer checks the equipment and conditions of the lungeing arena before work starts.

Leading the horse up to the lungeing ring
The side-reins should not be attached to the horse's head, as he may shy or be interfered with on the way to the ring, which could lead to an accident.

The loose end of the side-reins should be clipped on to

either the D-rings on the saddle or the ring on top of the roller, or clipped on to each other. There should be no untidy loops hanging down along the horse's sides, which could frighten him or catch on door handles etc.

The horse may be led off the lunge rein attached to the bridle or cavesson, with the lunge in the right hand, the lunge whip and thong in the left hand, the whip pointing backwards and downwards.

After arriving at the lungeing ring the horse should be positioned in the centre, and made to stand absolutely still so that the trainer can prepare him.

The trainer should always carry the lunge in his hand and should place the lunge whip under his arm. No matter how trustworthy the horse, he should never be left standing loose; prevention is better than cure.

The horse must be asked to stand still while he is made ready for lungeing. If the horse is excited and will not relax, ask an assistant to hold the horse. It is important for the horse's attitude to the work that he stands still, is relaxed and trusts the trainer. This trust, of course, will be undermined if the trainer uses rough checks on the lunge or a loud voice in order to get the horse to stand.

Preparation for lungeing and attaching the side-reins
Check that the girth and roller are tight enough and attach the side-reins. Shorten the side-reins gradually, especially with young horses – even the experienced horse should have fairly long side-reins when warming up.

Creating inward flexion by shortening the inside side-reins or lengthening the outside one is only done with the more advanced horse who has learned the beginnings of collection, lowering his haunches and carrying more weight behind. If the inside side-rein is shortened at an earlier stage in the training the horse loses his balance and starts to go crooked: the outside foreleg touches down a little more pronouncedly, the centre of gravity is shifted towards the outside shoulder, and the hind legs move outside the track of the forelegs.

The walk can be ruined if the horse is asked to walk for longer than two or three minutes in side-reins that are at a suitable length for trot and canter work. In walk the horse needs longer side-reins. It saves time to attach to the roller from the beginning an additional pair of side-reins adjusted to walking length. If the trainer changes pace to walk, he can simply unclip the trot-length side-reins and clip on the walking-length ones. The same procedure applies when changing from walk back to trot or canter. When not in use, the walk-length side-reins must be attached to the roller in such a way that they don't interfere with the horse's movement.

When the lunge is clipped on to the bit ring it must not be able to twist the ring, therefore it is clipped on below the spring-hook of the side-reins when these are in a high position; when the side-reins are in the normal position the lunge is clipped on above the spring-hook of the side-reins.

After all these preparations the work on the lunge can commence.

Starting to lunge

We start lungeing on the horse's softer side, which in most cases is on the left-hand rein.

The trainer holds the lunge in the left hand, with the spare line in loops, ready to slide freely out of the hand. The right hand holds the whip pointing behind the horse. The trainer stands beside the horse's shoulder, facing forwards. He asks the horse to move forward by leading with the lunge rein, using the voice and raising the point of the whip slightly.

The lunge is paid out slowly so that the trainer can control the horse and make sure that he moves off in walk. The horse should never be allowed to start trotting immediately or to rush off, but take care that he is not prevented from doing so with sharp turns as these can be harmful to the fetlock joints and can cause lameness.

After approximately two circuits the horse should have reached the outside track. To indicate to the horse that he should move towards the track, the trainer raises his left hand slightly and moves the point of the whip forward towards the quarters, or even towards the shoulder.

Since the side-reins are adjusted for trot work, the horse should not spend any more time in walk. He should be asked to trot on with the voice and a slight raising of the point of the whip. If the horse is reluctant to trot on, the whip aid is increased. The experienced trainer will touch the horse's hind leg just above the hock, with the end of the thong, at the moment when the horse's inside hind leg is on the ground. Thus he prevents the quarters from escaping outwards. The whip aid must always be supported by a short, sharp voice aid to teach the horse obedience. A little before and during the transition to trot the trainer takes up a slightly stronger contact on the lunge to give the horse inward flexion. The moment the horse moves into trot, the lunge is yielded but without losing the contact.

As a rule, the first trot session should last about five minutes to give the horse a chance to relax and get rid of any freshness.

The aid for the transition from trot to walk should be given clearly and always in the same manner. The main aid here is the voice, used in a soothing tone, and, if necessary, supported by a slight wave of the lunge. If the horse does not react promptly, the trainer has to remind his pupil by repeated taking and immediate giving on the lunge. The horse must not be allowed to increase his pace or take off and thereby risk injury.

The short 'taking' of the lunge rein achieves the best result if applied at the moment when the horse's inside foreleg is off the ground. When the foreleg touches down again, the lunge is yielded. The point of the whip remains lowered and may be moved forward towards the horse's shoulder to prevent the horse from coming into the centre. Also during the ensuing walk the horse should be kept out with this aid.

If necessary the length of the side-reins should be checked and adjusted.

After a short period in walk the horse is asked to strike off in canter. According to his stage of training this is done either from walk or from trot and is achieved by the voice and appropriate whip aid. Most horses find it easier to strike off from trot, which also has greater gymnasticising value.

To be able to make the transition from a rhythmic working trot, and not from an increasingly faster, running trot, the trainer has to have sufficient contact with the horse's mouth. Only during the first canter stride should the contact be eased again. For this transition use of controlled voice and whip aids, which must not frighten the horse, is important. The canter is maintained until rhythm and regular breathing are established.

Changing the rein
During the next short break at walk the rein is changed. To do this the horse is asked to halt on the track. If this cannot be achieved with voice, lunge and lowered whip, then the trainer should approach the horse from the front if possible, while shortening the lunge and sending half-halts down the lunge with wave movements. The horse must learn to halt on the track and not turn in to the centre. The horse will learn this quickly if the trainer rewards him each time. After adjusting the side-reins (if necessary) the trainer moves to the other side of the horse, changes the lunge rein on to the other bit ring (unless lungeing off the centre cavesson ring). The lunge rein

should be re-gathered correctly. As before, the trainer stands close to the horse, touches the horse gently with the whip just above the hock, and thus asks the horse to step round, as in a turn on the forehand, to change direction.

Once on the new rein the horse is asked to walk on. The trainer moves forward and sideways to take up position in the centre of the circle. He should watch the horse closely all the time and prevent him from turning around suddenly by using the whip in time and guiding the horse forward with the lunge.

When the rhythm is established in all three paces, on both reins, the trainer should start to work towards collection.

Depending on the horse's standard of training, the trainer may now shorten the side-reins and, if necessary, attach them to higher rings on the roller.

As work progresses the trainer will want the horse to carry more weight on his quarters. He will also want to see the haunches increasingly bent and the action more springy.

Through careful influence of the lunge and whip the strides are shortened, but they must maintain their activity and liveliness. Whilst the voice aid is still used, it plays more of a supporting role to the lunge and whip aids and is not used as an aid on its own.

In the early stages of teaching the horse to collect his strides, ask for collection for just two or three circuits then lengthen the strides before asking for collection again.

At first work on collection is practised in trot, then also in canter. At a later stage frequent changes from one pace to another should be made. The walk, and only with lengthened side-reins, is practised during the short rest periods.

When the horse's gymnasticising has advanced considerably, the trainer can increase collection by making the circle gradually smaller, to about 10 m diameter, but it has to be increased again when making transitions into medium and fairly extended paces.

After five to ten minutes' work the rein is changed. In total the lungeing session should not be more than thirty or forty minutes.

Finishing the lungeing session
After a final break in walk, with the side-reins either lengthened or removed, the horse is again asked to halt on the track, and the trainer approaches, gathering in the lunge rein. The whip is carried under the left arm so that the hands are free to disengage the side-reins and loosen the noseband and the roller etc. The trainer should never forget to reward the horse after the work.

Trainer and horse should leave the lungeing arena in the same manner as they approached it (as described earlier).

4.2 Lungeing young horses

Usually, the young horse's serious training starts on the lunge.

The final value of the horse can depend on the way in which the horse is familiarised with saddle and bridle and thereafter with the rider's weight. It is logical, therefore, that this important first phase of the horse's education is handled by experts with plenty of experience in lungeing older, trained horses.

As a rule the following steps describe the early phases of the training but adaptations may have to be made to suit individual circumstances.

Making the horse familiar with the surroundings
If at all possible this should be done with free exercise in an indoor school or (fenced-in) outdoor arena.

Making the horse familiar with the equipment
As soon as possible, after the horse has been loosened up in free exercise, he should be made familiar with saddle and bridle. The more carefully and calmly that this is done, the quicker the horse will accept them. To prevent accidents it is advisable to have an assistant when tacking up.

The trainer should not introduce the horse to the lunge until the pupil has accepted the tack without resistance or tension when being led on a lead rein. The practice of letting the horse buck can easily lead to injuries and is not recommended.

If the horse is allowed time to become familiar with this new aspect of life, the trainer will be repaid by much quicker progress later on.

The equipment for the first lungeing session is:

☐ A sturdy bridle, minus its reins, and a drop noseband.

☐ A cavesson (it is not advisable to use a headcollar, but if it is the only equipment available, it must fit tightly).

☐ A saddle, stirrups taken off; and a surcingle to keep the saddle flaps down.

☐ Bandages or boots, at least for the front legs. If the horse is shod behind, hind boots should be worn.

Since the horse does not wear side-reins during the initial stages, it is important that the lungeing ring is as near perfect as possible (see Chapter 2). It cannot be said often enough that the erection of a surrounding barrier is vitally important for this early work.

The following are the steps for the first lunge lessons.

The first lunge lesson
If help is available, an assistant leads the horse on the track of the circle, walking beside the horse on its inside and

behind the lunge rein. The helper should not interfere with the lunge. At first the trainer also moves on a circle but further from the horse, then takes up his position in the centre. The hand holding the lunge rein stays a little in advance of the horse. The whip encourages forward motion but at first only in walk. The horse should not get excited.

Once the horse is walking along the track in a relaxed manner the helper can let go and move towards the centre of the circle. He then stands behind the trainer, taking care not to interfere with the whip. The horse can then be asked to trot, encouraged by the voice.

The trainer should endeavour to maintain a light contact all the time. The horse has to learn to move in an even rhythm along the track, inside the barrier. It does not matter if the lunge sometimes hangs rather loose, in a loop, as long as it does not touch the ground. If the horse falls in, the trainer points the whip towards the shoulder to make him go out to the track again.

If the horse has worked satisfactorily for fifteen minutes, change the rein. Again, the assistant leads the horse at first.

The initial work on the lunge should not be continued for more than thirty minutes.

If there is no help available, the trainer leads the horse on the track with his right hand and gradually moves away from the horse, paying out the lunge. At first, the rolled-up lunge and the whip, pointing backwards, are carried in the left hand, then the whip is changed to the right hand.

During this first phase of the lungeing exercise it is important that the horse becomes confident in the work and moves calmly in walk and trot on the track.

During the first few days it is advisable to ask for only a quiet working trot, without looking for 'schwung' or overtracking. If the horse offers to canter, this can be allowed, as long as the trainer remains in control. Rushing off must not be permitted as there is danger of the horse falling or injuring himself. If necessary, the trainer may have to shorten the lunge and move forward towards the horse and regain control with determined aids.

During the first training phase all aids have to be given very precisely. The command to trot on should be given in a short, determined voice together with a slight raising of the point of the whip and a slight increase in tension on the lunge, created by turning the wrist.

The aids for a downwards transition are applied with the same determination. The whip is obviously lowered, but still pointed towards the horse's quarters.

To slow the pace the trainer uses his voice in long-drawn-out, soothing words. In addition the tension on the lunge is increased at the moment the inside foreleg is lifted, and decreased at the moment the leg touches down again. If the horse makes no attempt to obey these aids, the trainer must immediately reapply them, but much more strongly. A continual weak aid only confirms in the horse's mind the concept that he is the boss, an idea which makes later training much more difficult. On the other hand, when the horse obeys, the trainer must be generous in his praise.

After three or four days the horse should be fairly familiar with the lungeing process. The trainer can then introduce the side-reins. Working for too long a period without side-reins will make the horse fall on to the outside shoulder and this has no educational value; it is merely a damaging exercise.

The horse must be able to find a contact when he starts to drop his head and neck to look for it. The trainer should assess the horse's skeletal frame and muscles to help him decide when, how long and how high to adjust the side-reins. The natural posture of the horse while moving must not be interfered with. The aim is for the outside side-rein to provide a definite contact when neck and back muscles are extended.

Too deep a head position, where the mouth is below the horizontal line through the elbow, brings the horse too much on to the forehand and blocks the bending of the haunches.

The trainer should not try to counteract this deep head position by fixing the side-reins higher, but should attach them at the desired height between point of shoulder and elbow, and correct the head and neck position with forward driving aids. It is easy for these aids to produce a quicker tempo but the forwardness has to be converted into greater activity of the hind legs, which then step closer to the centre of gravity. Speed is certainly not required. The trainer has to dampen excessive pushing power with half-halts, delivered at the correct moment, i.e. when the inside foreleg is being lifted.

To help the horse receive the half-halts attach the lunge rein to the cavesson so that its influence is felt on the nasal bone. If the trainer is experienced, however, and the work is progressing well, the lunge can be attached to the inside bit ring, but at first only in conjunction with the cheek-piece of the noseband. The outside side-rein will give the lunge rein a counterweight, even if the lunge is used with increased tension, especially if the lungeing ring has a suitable barrier.

If the horse carries his head and neck too high, the back will drop and the back muscles will be unable to work. The trainer should not make the mistake of adjusting the side-reins to a lower position or of attaching them to the girth between the horse's forelegs. Neither would offer the solution to this problem.

The correct remedy is to attach the side-reins to the roller at a medium height, and allow the horse to move rather slowly and lazily until he lowers the neck. Then, one can start to apply forward driving aids, creating more activity and thus teaching the horse to look for a contact in the desired frame.

The Lauffer rein (discussed in Chapter 2) can be useful in the early stages of the horse's training. With this rein the bit ring cannot be pulled backwards when a horse tries to go deeper, as is the case with side-reins.

At this initial stage of training it would be very wrong to use the 'over head' lunge or a check-rein to keep the horse's head and front up, as this blocks the activity of the back muscles.

During the first four to six weeks of training the horse is usually backed, but the training on the lunge continues for two to three months. During this time evidence of the progressive gymnastic training will be apparent in the muscles of the horse's buttocks and on the top of his neck. But the most important aspect of the training on the lunge is the development and maintenance of a good rhythm, relaxation and activity in the horse's movement.

4.3 Lungeing an advanced horse

During the more advanced training of the horse, lungeing may be used to improve collection. A pre-condition for achieving this is that the trainer has a schooled eye. Looking at the horse's conformation he must decide to what degree of collection and bending of the haunches each horse is capable. Any over-working or incorrect work will quickly lead to resistance and can even damage the horse physically.

Used correctly, the following will assist the trainer in his work:

The check-rein
This should always be used in conjunction with a cavesson

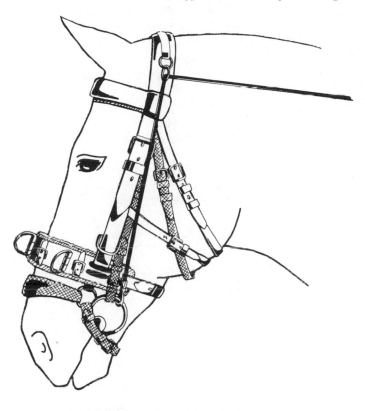

14. Attaching the check-rein.

that is fitted with leather pads to protect the horse's head against the pressure of the check-rein. The rings on the headpiece of the cavesson, through which the check-rein is fed, must be attached close to the headpiece, otherwise the check-rein cannot apply its elevating effect and the rings could also rub and injure the horse's eye.

Whenever a check-rein, or any other rein designed to raise the horse's head, is used, the trainer should ensure, first and foremost, that the movement of the horse's back muscles is not blocked. These reins are designed to prevent the horse from carrying his head too deep, not to lift the head up. Any rein with a similar effect to the check-rein will only be effective if the trainer activates the horse's quarters.

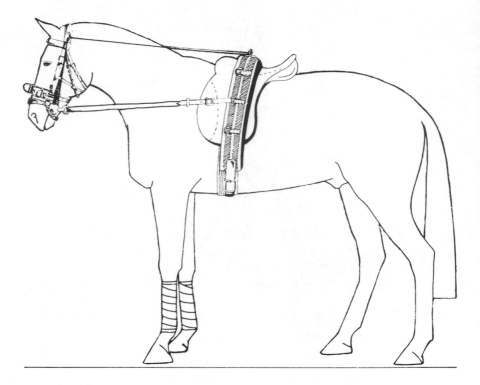

*15. A horse tacked up for lungeing and fitted
with a check-rein.*

The trainer can gymnasticise the horse and improve
collection without using any of these auxiliary reins, by
choosing the right pace, using a lot of transitions and by
temporarily decreasing the diameter of the circle. The
trainer then uses the ordinary side-rein, but attached to a
higher ring on the side of the roller. The horse's mouth
should be approximately on the same horizontal line as the
hip joint. The nasal bone is carried vertically when the
side-reins are attached, and the horse is standing. With
correct forward driving aids the nose will then be slightly
in front of the vertical when the horse moves. The poll
should always be the highest point.

The trainer keeps up the activity by use of voice and by

touching the hind fetlocks with the end of the thong at the moment when they are leaving the ground. At the same time he controls the forward movement with half-halts. The diameter of the circle can be varied by shortening the lunge rein and then lengthening it again. While the circle is smaller the whip touches the horse's buttocks, causing the inside hind leg to cross over slightly. This shortened trot or canter should not be done for longer than one or two circles.

The shortening is followed by an increase in the circle's diameter, when the trainer asks the horse to increase the length of stride.

The transitions within a pace give the opportunity to judge the horse's suppleness and obedience. This type of

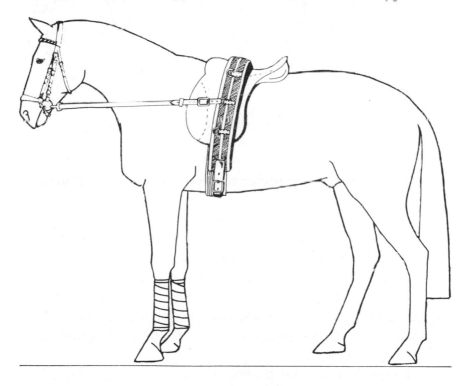

16. Attaching the side-reins. The horse's mouth is level with his hip.

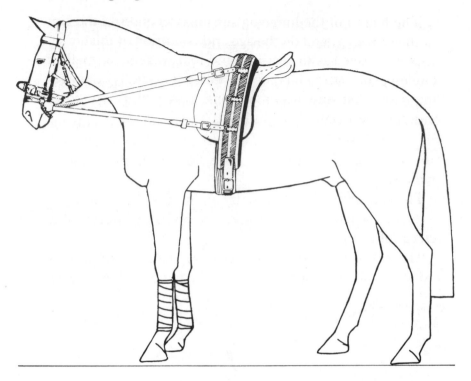

17. *The Lauffer rein can be adjusted at various heights.*

work, if executed conscientiously, advances the training considerably.

As before a trainer should not work for long periods in walk on the lunge, and when he does the side-reins must be lengthened and the check-rein taken off.

Frequent changes of rein give the trainer the opportunity to adjust the side-reins, to touch the horse's quarters with the whip and ask the horse to step around with the inside hind leg crossing over, thus preparing for the work in-hand.

Depending on the degree of collection achieved, the inside side-rein may be shortened by one or two holes to give the horse a little flexion.

The length of the lungeing sessions depends on the aim of the lungeing, and on the age and condition of the horse. However, one has to bear in mind that work on a smallish circle is very strenuous for the horse. Generally, a lungeing session should never be longer than thirty to forty minutes, rest periods included.

5. Work over cavaletti and fences

Cavaletti and poles acquaint the horse with obstacles on the ground. They improve the horse's sureness of foot and suppleness. During lungeing, cavaletti and poles can be very helpful in positioning a horse for a fence and as a ground-line.

When training young horses loss of balance will be the biggest problem, and this has to be overcome before demands can be increased. The young horse finds his balance easier on a straight line than on a circle. This also applies on the lungeing circle, although here the horse is not interfered with by the rider's weight. For this reason lungeing over cavaletti should not be introduced at the beginning of the training on the lunge.

With an experienced horse, lunge work over cavaletti improves relaxation and rhythm, and the taking of higher steps will develop muscles. If the work is carried out progressively it can improve the horse's action and cadence.

Using cavaletti on the lunge too early, especially if the distances are not adjusted to the individual horse, can cause injuries like splints and sprains.

Lungeing over cavaletti in a permanent lungeing ring is not advisable because there is nowhere to set up the obstacles except on the track. It is better, therefore, to lunge in an open space, or at least one that is open on one side, so that the cavaletti can be laid out separately. When lungeing in between the cavaletti exercises, there will be no barrier or fence on the outside and therefore this work can only be done with horses whose lunge work is established.

The trainer will need a minimum of three cavaletti, a

maximum of six, arranged on the curve of a circle, fanning out from the centre, the middle of the poles offering the normal distance. This gives the trainer the opportunity to choose the distance he thinks suitable at any time. On the outside the fence around the lungeing ring acts as a jump wing; on the inside a pole on top of the crosses of the cavaletti makes sure that the lunge cannot get caught.

If work over the cavaletti is intensified and carried out in all three paces, it is advisable to have one lungeing ring

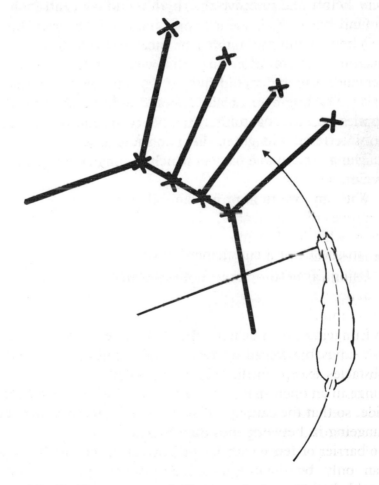

18. *Setting up cavaletti on a circle, with poles on the inside.*

free of any poles or cavaletti in the centre, and adjoining circles with cavaletti set up at walk, trot and canter distances (walk–80 cm; trot–1.2 m; and canter–3.5 m). Since all cavaletti are set up fanwise, it is possible to vary the distances slightly by decreasing or increasing the size of the circle.

Work over the cavaletti is started very gradually. First, only one cavaletti is placed on the track, then three. Two cavaletti would make the horse jump, whereas three invite him to trot and improve the rhythm and concentration.

Only when the horse is happy and confident over three cavaletti should the number be increased, ultimately to a maximum of six. More than this would be too strenuous for the horse and would induce tension instead of relaxation. Walking over cavaletti should only be done rarely, in which case it is absolutely necessary to remove the side-reins or at least lengthen them considerably.

The most suitable pace in which to lunge over cavaletti is the trot.

The aims are to improve the following:

☐ Concentration.

☐ Relaxation and engagement of the back.

☐ Rhythm, balance and sureness of foot.

☐ Collection and cadence.

When working to achieve the first three aims, the side-reins are lengthened by two or three holes and attached one ring deeper on the side of the roller.

It is important that in the beginning the horse is led into and over the cavaletti. This is more effective than an uncontrolled driving into the obstacle.

Especially important is the correct speed of the pace (tempo). Most people make the mistake of going too fast, which does not improve relaxation but tenses up the back. On the other hand, going too slowly can cause the horse to

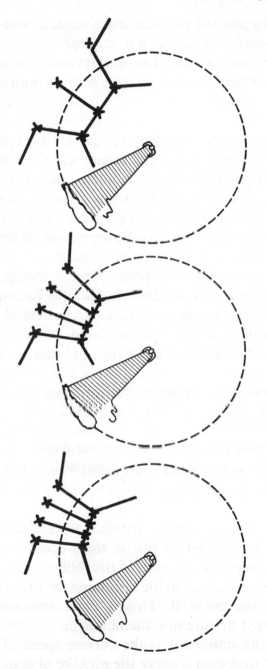

**19. Various set-ups with different distances for
all three paces.**

lose his rhythm and put in an extra stride or step on top of a pole, possibly resulting in an injury.

Correct use of the whip is important in this work, especially when the cavaletti are used to improve collection and cadence.

When working on collection, the side-reins remain at their usual length, but they should not be attached too high. When working over higher cavaletti there is a greater danger of the horse hollowing his back.

During this collection work the distances between the cavaletti may be shortened slightly, whereas they can be lengthened slightly when working towards relaxation.

The height of the cavaletti depends on the horse's degree of training and the object of the lungeing. As a rule the lowest height – 10 cm – is chosen. To improve the horse's alertness, when working over a row of cavaletti, one or two cavaletti can be raised to 20 cm. Very experienced trainers sometimes work with cavaletti at 30 cm when improving their horses' collection.

Now and again cavaletti set at their maximum height of 45–50 cm are used when working in canter.

When working over cavaletti in canter the aim is for the horse to find the right take-off point and to cope with related distances between obstacles. Young horses canter over cavaletti as an introduction to jumping; older horses can improve their use of the back. This work can culminate in jumping a horse over fences up to 1.2 m high.

As a general rule jumping on the lunge should be kept to a minimum. When jumping on the lunge, even over small fences, the danger of injuries is very much greater, as the inward pull of the lunge can force the inside foreleg to twist, turning the fetlock joint and pedal bone. Jumping training without the rider, like loose-jumping in an indoor school or fenced-in outdoor arena, is preferable to jumping on the lunge.

Jumping on the lunge should only be done over fixed

fences. On the outside of the fence there must be a wing, and the inside must be constructed so as to allow the lunge to glide easily over the edge of the fence. Side-reins should be removed.

Do not construct jumps out of cavaletti placed on top of one another. If the horse makes a mistake the lunge could get caught on the inside crosses, even if they are protected by a 'gliding' pole. Any falling fence material could easily get between the horse's legs.

6. Lungeing for special purposes

In this chapter the following specialisations are considered:

☐ Preparatory work shortly before a competition.
☐ Improving the rider's seat.
☐ Vaulting.

In all cases the horse must be well used to work on the lunge, but the type of equipment and technique used will vary depending on the purpose of the lungeing.

Lungeing before a competition

Very rarely is there enough room in the warming-up area to allow the rider to lunge in peace and not interfere with others. However, if it is necessary to lunge a horse to loosen it up before a competition the rider should always respect other competitors and look for a quiet corner, preferably with at least one side separated by a barrier.

Since the task of lungeing before a competition is often done by an assistant, it is necessary to give him precise instructions. Trotting or cantering around wildly without side-reins is useless and counterproductive. The horse should be tacked up properly with side-reins. If proper lungeing equipment is not available, attach the ends of the reins to the girth. Roll up the stirrups to prevent them from flapping.

For shows and travelling a lunge whip which can be taken apart in the middle is useful.

Improving the rider's seat

An important consideration when lungeing a rider to improve his position is the choice of a suitable horse. When lungeing a beginner or teaching an advanced rider feel, the trainer needs a well-schooled horse with a suitable temperament.

When lungeing a beginner, the horse should be tacked up with side-reins attached to the bit rings, which will place the horse's head and neck and make his back work. When improving a rider's seat and feel one should use the best-trained horse available.

The trainer uses the whip and lunge in the same manner as in ordinary lungeing.

Vaulting

A vaulting horse has to be specially trained to listen to the trainer's voice and to respond to subtle signals from the whip.

Use of the 'over-head' lungeing method is not recommended in vaulting but this has to be mentioned here because some not-so-experienced trainers use it to raise the horse's head, but all they do is break the rhythm of the canter and hollow the horse's back. It is also wrong to shorten one side-rein in order to keep the horse on the track.

These practices lead to faults which can become well-established because the trainer cannot pay so much attention to the horse while concentrating on the athletes. If this happens the vaulting horse has to be taken away from this kind of work and reschooled by an expert.

7. The double lunge

Lungeing a horse in the double lunge is done for several reasons:

☐ To provide advanced training after the ordinary work on the lunge.

☐ For working difficult horses who will benefit from the control of an outside lunge rein.

☐ As preparation for high-school movements.

☐ As preparation for driving.

Equipment and techniques

Before starting the work with the double lunge the horse must be schooled on the single lunge first. As before, the horse's legs should be protected.

The equipment is the same as for lungeing on a single lunge rein, except that side-reins are omitted. For this work, however, the roller must have large rings, 5–10 cm in diameter. A light breastplate, as used in driving, can be useful as it has rings on the neckstrap through which the lunge can be fed on each side, before passing through the lower ring on the side of the roller. This has the advantage that the double lunge acts in the direction of the rider's reins and that the lungeing induces a deeper position, which makes it easier to control the horse's lateral bend.

The double lunge rein should have a total length of 16–17 m and be all one piece, so that there is no buckle in the way of the trainer's hands. It is also advantageous if the first 2 m at each end are round-stitched, so that the lunge will glide through the rings more easily.

It is best to use a single lunge rein, but if a long enough one is not available, it is possible to make do with two

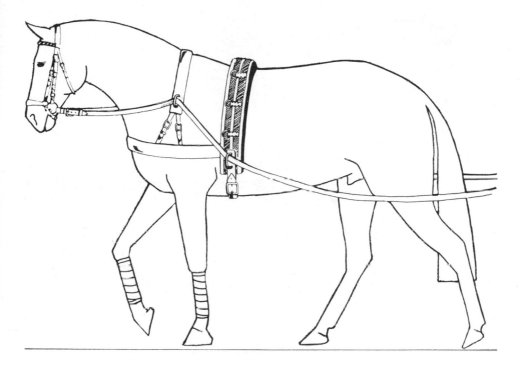

20. Attaching the double lunge with a harness breastplate.

standard lunge reins. However, the trainer has then to put up with the inconvenience of the join. If working off a bridle, the ends of the double lunge are clipped or buckled on to the bit rings. If working off a cavesson, the two side rings are used. If there is no roller and/or driving harness available, one can improvise by adjusting the stirrups at the desired height, and securing them with a strap passing under the belly.

Even if the horse has been trained on the ordinary lunge, it is advisable to have an assistant when starting the work with the double lunge. After the initial lessons the trainer can manage alone.

At first one has to familiarise the horse with the feeling of the outside lunge touching his legs. The horse is

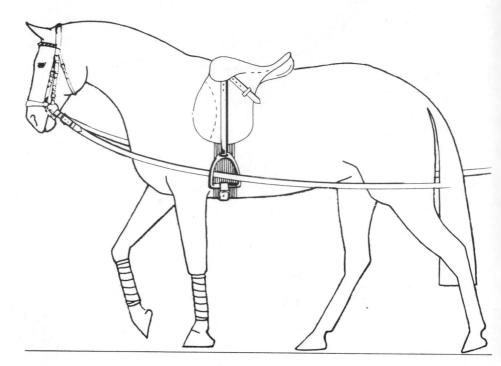

21. The stirrups can be secured underneath the horse and used as makeshift roller rings for the double lunge.

warmed up with the single lunge. Then the assistant holds the horse, standing behind the inside lunge rein. The outside lunge is then attached and the trainer slides it carefully over the horse's croup down to a point which is just a hand above his hocks. If the horse accepts this calmly, the assistant can lead him to the track. The helper can then work his way to the centre and take up his position behind the trainer.

It is the assistant's task to keep the horse going forward with the whip, while the trainer holds the inside lunge as usual in his left hand, and the outside lunge in his right hand. The loop at the end is held with the little finger of the right hand.

The assistant should continue to hold the whip until the horse becomes used to the double lunge when moving. Later on the trainer will be able to hold the lunge reins and the whip and co-ordinate the aids.

When lungeing on the left-hand rein, the trainer should hold the left lunge between the thumb and forefinger of his left hand, with the outside (right) lunge between the middle and ring finger. The right hand is then free to help adjust the lunge reins, and to work the whip correctly without interfering with the horse's mouth.

On the right-hand rein, both lunges are held in the right hand: the inside (right) lunge is held between the middle and ring finger and the left (outside) lunge runs over the index finger and the back of the hand. The left hand holds the whip and adjusts the lunge reins if necessary.

The outside lunge must always lie above the hock, otherwise the moving leg will interfere with the horse's mouth and cause the horse to kick.

In the early stages of double-lunge training or when the horse is still fresh, it is possible that he will kick. The trainer then needs the assistant to help make the horse go forward. If the horse is allowed to stop and possibly to turn around, a precarious situation can arise, which can only be remedied with calmness and by leading the horse back on to the track. Sensitive horses can become very upset, and the trainer should consider if this work is necessary and if it would not be better to go back to the single lunge and re-establish the basics.

In principle the double lunge is worked the same way as the single lunge. Depending on the aims, the relaxing work or the collecting work will be dominant. The advantage of the double lunge, however, is that the more-or-less dead contact of the side-reins is replaced by the direct contact with both sides of the horse's mouth and the trainer's hands, which can, of course, be much softer.

The trainer also can influence the flexion and bend at

the right moment.

As a rule the outside lunge has a controlling function. It should never be pulled so tight that the movement is interfered with and the quarters are pushed inwards.

A further advantage of the double lunge is the fact that one can change the rein without halting and switch paces without the time-consuming changing of the side-reins.

With training, the horse will be able to change the rein in all three paces and perform flying changes at canter.

Depending on the horse's stage of training and the room available, there are two ways of changing the rein: on a long line – changing 'out of the circle'; on a tight turn – changing 'through the circle'.

In the first case, the trainer leaves his position the moment the horse reaches the changing point, and then follows the horse to the centre of the new circle. To achieve the change the trainer lengthens the new outside lunge and shortens the new inside lunge as the horse arrives at the changing points. As both lunges are held in one hand the other hand is free to adjust the length of the lunges.

The whip points backwards whilst not in use, but it should be kept ready for use as needed. Changing the lunges – and the whip – from one hand to the other needs some practice.

It is very important to lengthen the new outside lunge sufficiently, otherwise the horse cannot bend into the new direction or may even go in the wrong direction.

When changing the rein 'through' the circle, the outside lunge is lengthened and then the inside one is shortened to bring the horse into the circle.

The trainer lengthens the new outside lunge by approximately 3 m and shortens the new inside lunge accordingly. He then steps behind the horse and directs him, on an S-shaped line, to the track of the new circle. At the same time both lunges and the whip change hands simultaneously.

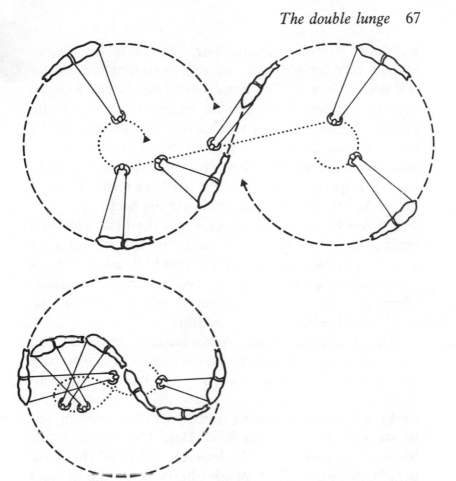

22. *Changing the rein with the double lunge 'out of the circle' and 'through the circle'.*

As the standard of training and experience improves, the influence of the outside lunge becomes more and more important. In the early stages of training, the outside rein is used mainly for control. As the training advances, the contact on the outside rein becomes more positive, but always in conjunction with the necessary forward driving aids from voice and whip. The horse should 'seek' this intensified outside contact by stretching along his outside. This will give him the desired 'relative lifting of the forehand' (German: *Aufrichtung*). For this the trainer needs a very feeling hand – merely lightening the contact will not achieve it. The horse has to be pushed forward into the contact, and when he accepts it the hands are yielded slightly, inviting the horse to follow and stretch forwards and down. The type of horse and its conformation determine the degree of lengthening in the neck, but it is important that the horse stretches forward, out of the back, and does not merely lower his neck.

Too deep a head position prevents the hind legs from coming under the body sufficiently, towards the centre of gravity. The deepest position that should be allowed is one where the horse's nose is in line with his point of shoulder-elbow line. In the more advanced collecting work, the nose should be in line with the hip.

The actual work on the double lunge is the same as on the single lunge and includes transitions from pace to pace and transitions within the pace, as well as frequent changes of rein, flexion and bend. As a preparation for working in-hand to achieve collection, the horse can also be worked on a straight line. Here the trainer walks behind the horse, at a safe distance, 'framing' the horse with both lunges. It is mainly the voice or the in-hand work whip (see later) that is used to shorten and lengthen the horse's steps.

The double lunge also offers a chance to teach the horse leg-yielding and, later on, other lateral movements. To start with, it is advisable to work alongside the kicking-boards or the surrounding fence of the arena. It is important that the trainer watches the horse's reactions, and that he moves with the horse and is not dragged along by the lunges. With good feel in the hands he establishes the tempo, flexion and bend.

The trainer must be aware that this work is only a preparation for work in-hand and he should not expect a perfect performance.

8. Improving collection with work in-hand

With some horses the training under the rider can be supplemented with work in-hand, as long as there has been training on the lunge and sufficient gymnasticisation.

The collecting work in-hand improves the horse's understanding of the forward driving and slowing down aids. He learns, without the rider's weight, to go forward on to the bit, 'bounce' back and lighten, thereby lowering the haunches. With the whip the horse is encouraged to bring his hind legs closer to the centre of gravity, and with the aid of half-halts from the trainer's hand, he learns to lower his haunches, give in the poll and to develop more self-carriage. This improves the horse's posture which in turn benefits the work under the rider.

Also, the trainer (rider) learns through this work to improve the feel in his hands and to understand more about collection.

Practising collection in-hand should only be done as part of advanced training. It is, however, suitable for horses who have difficulties under the rider and who are too weak to collect sufficiently or who have conformational deficiencies. Collective work in-hand in these cases can be more beneficial than prolonged work under the rider, because it is easier to avoid overworking when practising work in-hand.

In-hand work is also useful for younger horses as they can learn to carry themselves in a good shape more easily and quickly than when having to cope with the weight of the rider. It also improves the horse's temperament; nervous horses can be made more trusting to the hand, and lazy ones a little more alert.

To practise the work in-hand one needs a location similar to that for lungeing. The equipment should consist of:

☐ Bridle with noseband – possibly a lunge.

☐ Saddle with surcingle.

☐ Side-reins.

☐ Boots or bandages, ideally for all four legs.

☐ Lead rein or lunge rein.

The trainer also needs a special whip, at least 1.5 m long, strong and springy, and for safety reasons good footwear (no spurs) and gloves.

Use of the equipment depends on the aim of the work. The various steps are:

1. To familiarise the horse with the work in-hand – and as a rule this is done in association with lungeing.

2. To start lowering the haunches, and become lighter while moving in half-steps forward.

3. To achieve pronounced collection with suitable higher carriage and the development of rhythmic steps of piaffe, nearly on the spot, to gymnasticise the haunches.

The first aim is closely related to the work on the lunge.

When changing the rein, the trainer has a chance to move the horse's forehand around on a very small circle and to let the quarters move around on a bigger circle, similar to a turn around the forehand. The horse learns here to tolerate both being touched with the whip as a forward driving aid and the trainer's restriction on the bit to keep him from moving forward too much.

To start the collecting work in-hand the horse is taken to the track along the wall for short periods during a lungeing session. The trainer gathers up the lunge and holds the rein about one hand's width away from the clip or buckle fastening. A cavesson is useful for this as it reduces the interference. It also gives the trainer a better chance to control a horse with half-halts on the nasal bone. The trainer stands beside the horse's head, in front of the left shoulder, and faces the horse's quarters. Moving backwards himself, he takes the horse forward a short step. The whip, held in the right hand, causes the horse to move forward with a touch between hock and buttocks.

If a longer period of work in-hand is planned it is advisable to exchange the lunge whip for the work in-hand whip.

The first task is to teach the horse to carry more weight behind through lowering the quarters and by moving forward in half-steps. The aids should be well balanced between forward and restricting ones, the voice (clicking) and the whip helping this aim. At first the horse might try to escape by dashing forwards. If the trainer anticipates this, he should lengthen the lunge and let the horse move around him on a small circle, 8 m in diameter. When the horse relaxes he can be repositioned along the kicking boards. It is important that these first exercises always start off from a halt.

A frequent mistake is to pull the horse's head inwards, away from the wall. This is seen with less experienced trainers. It is important, therefore, to remain beside the horse's head. Also, stronger contact on the outside rein can improve the horse's straightness. The trainer should not think about achieving piaffe.

The work is done for short periods only and must be interspersed with lungeing sessions in free trot and canter on the track of the lungeing ring. After achieving a few cadenced steps advancing about 0.6–1 m, one should stop. In total, the work should not extend beyond thirty or forty minutes, only one third of it being collecting work in-hand, the rest consisting of normal lungeing at a freer pace.

The rein is changed only after the horse has worked satisfactorily on the easy rein (usually the left one).

In the second training aim clearly marked short steps with lowered haunches are sought – but not piaffe. The horse is working well if a cadenced trot stride covers 30–60 cm and the horse stands calmly 'on the bit' (nasal bone in front of the vertical, poll the highest point). The smallest success must immediately be rewarded by a break, praise and leading the horse at walk.

It is advisable to start this work after only brief warming up. The warming up can be done by free exercise or a few minutes' riding. After not more than twenty minutes of the collecting work in-hand, check by riding that the horse is learning to collect.

For the first stages, the equipment for the work in-hand is the same as for lungeing. A saddle should always be used together with a roller, so that stability is given to the side-reins and to safeguard the desired effect of the horse becoming lighter on the bit. It is advisable to attach the lunge or lead rein to the cavesson, but if the trainer's hand has enough feel the lunge can be attached to the bridle.

In the second stage it should be possible to work the horse on the stiffer side, and this should be in the ratio of 2:1 (softer side 2, stiffer side 1).

The third stage of collecting work in-hand can only be started if aims 1 and 2 have been achieved satisfactorily. It is unpractical and damaging to require a higher degree of collection from the horse without having gymnasticised the haunches first.

The horse's behaviour and his ability to learn in the first two stages will determine the procedure in the third stage. If the horse has co-operated well or sufficiently, then it is advisable for the trainer to proceed alone, as this will help the co-ordination of the aids. The aim is now to advance from the half-steps forward to an increasing number of piaffe steps which hardly cover any ground. It is absolutely imperative that the trainer, with slightly lifting half-halts, ensures that the horse is not looking for increased contact on the side-reins for support and 'pushes himself' forward. He should, however, carry himself with marked raising of the forehand (*aufrichtung*), a soft mouth and a swinging back.

During this training the horse should become more sensitive and attentive to the aids. It is therefore the trainer's task to respond with delicate, well-timed aids, given in the correct place and at the correct time.

The whip, supported by the voice, can be used by holding it on the horse's side, or 'touching' the horse to produce varying effects.

Using the whip near the fetlocks will, as a rule, cause more pronounced lifting of the hinds, whereas, if used higher between the hock and buttocks it will cause forward movement.

Touching with the whip will cause the following effects:

☐ On the front of the forearm or on the knee – a more pronounced action of the forearm and shoulder.

☐ On the front of the fetlock – a slight lifting of the leg.

☐ On the shoulder or forearm – return the forehand in line with the quarters.

☐ On the side of the quarters – a forward crossing and a lowering of the haunches to produce a little more activity of the hind legs.

☐ On the back of the buttock – an increased lifting and forward movement of the hind leg by increasing flexion of the hock.

☐ On the back of the hind cannon – increased activity by flexion of the hock joint.

☐ On the back of the hind fetlock or the ball of the hind hoof – an increased stepping forward.

☐ On the croup – with some horses a lowering of the croup and quarters and a raising of the forehand; with others a backwards kick.

In this phase of the training the collecting work in-hand is practised equally on both reins. If the horse has achieved twenty to thirty rhythmic and cadenced piaffe steps it is time to put a light rider into the saddle. He must sit perfectly still and, at first, give no aids at all. He is merely a 'weight' to teach the horse to carry a rider in this high degree of collection. In future work, the rider can gradually take over and give the aids and the trainer moves more and more into the background.

If a horse, in spite of correct preparation, continually tries to escape forward, then it is advisable to work with an assistant. The helper should stand in front of the horse on the track and lead him on the lunge or lead rein, moving backwards only slightly and only if necessary. (A lead rein may only be used on a cavesson.)

He must restrain the horse's forward movement as far as necessary, without interfering with the rhythm. The trainer can now, standing slightly more backwards – halfway along the horse – push him forward. Co-ordination between the two people is important so that good forward driving aids are not suffocated by incorrectly applied half-halts. On the other hand, the horse must also respect the assistant so that he learns not to escape the collection by dashing forward.

The collecting work in-hand in half-steps and piaffe steps is followed by the development of the passage.

To achieve this the collection is first improved by touching with the whip in the upper leg region, and then the horse is 'let out' on the lead rein in rhythmic passage steps on the straight line of the track.

Tactful touching of the back of the knee or the muscle above it can improve the action of the forelegs.

How strongly the aids should be applied is decided by the horse's temperament. One should always try to use the lightest possible aid. Continual voice and whip aids make the horse dull and slow to react.

The collecting work in-hand can also be used during short breaks in the training under the rider when they are used as revision sessions.

There is no need for any special equipment. It is sufficient if the rider rolls up the stirrups so that they cannot disturb the horse.

The horse stands on the track with the rider positioned on the inside, beside his head, facing the horse's quarters.

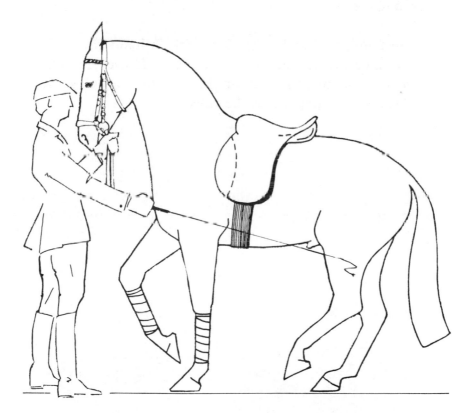

*23. Working in-hand with a trained horse during a
break in a ridden schooling session.*

The outside rein is placed over the horse's neck about two hands' width behind the ears, and is pulled through the inside bit ring so that a contact is taken up. The end of the rein is folded back and upwards, placed on the other half of the rein and held in one hand. The same hand also holds the inside rein so that it does not dangle down. A horse which has become established in his in-hand work may be held as shown in Fig. 23. The other hand holds the whip, as usual. The rein hand, which is held cheekbone high, close to the horse's head, must have feel and try to stay 'in front of the horse's mouth'. By turning the wrist, the rider can influence the inside or the outside rein when holding the reins as described.

Correct lungeing and collecting work in-hand can be of great value in the training of the horse. However, every trainer must be conscious of the fact that nothing can replace the training under the rider.

Index